SOLAR
POWER

© Aladdin Books Ltd

Designed and produced by
Aladdin Books Ltd
70 Old Compton St
London W1

*First published in the
United States 1985 by*
Gloucester Press
387 Park Avenue South
New York, 10016

Library of Congress
Catalog Card No. 85-70599

ISBN 0531 170063

Printed in Belgium

The cover shows an infra-red photograph of
heat differences on the sun's surface.

Photographic credits:
Cover, McClancy Collection/NASA; page 4/5,
Tony Stone Associates; pages 6/7, 21 and 22,
Frank Spooner; pages 9 and 10, Friends of the
Earth; pages 12, 19 and 25, Zefa; pages 15
and 17, Sandia Laboratories; page 23, SERI.

ROBIN McKIE

Illustrated by
Ron Hayward Associates

Consultant
Stewart Boyle

Gloucester Press
New York : Toronto

Introduction

Our lives depend on energy. We need it to heat our homes, to make electricity and to move us around on land and in the air.

Most energy is derived from the sun. For instance, coal is made from ancient plants that needed the sun's heat and light to grow. But the sun's rays can also be turned directly into electricity and new types of fuels. All these forms of "solar energy" are being developed, and many remote places which do not have electricity may soon benefit from solar power.

The sun: fifteen million degrees Celsius!

Contents

Energy from the sun

There are many ways of capturing the energy of the sun's rays. In "passive" heating, buildings are designed to simply trap the sun's heat. In "active" heating, sunlight is gathered up by collectors such as the huge reflecting mirrors below, and converted to hot water and electricity.

Solar energy is free and will never run out. Many people around the world – in both poor developing countries and rich western nations – want to use it for their energy needs.

Solar reflecting mirrors in the Californian desert

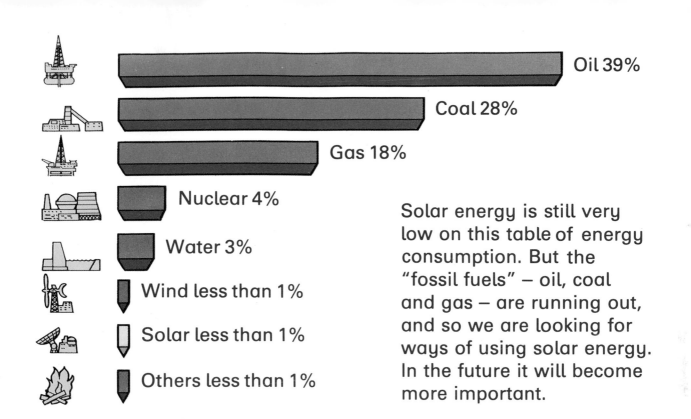

Oil 39%

Coal 28%

Gas 18%

Nuclear 4%

Water 3%

Wind less than 1%

Solar less than 1%

Others less than 1%

Solar energy is still very low on this table of energy consumption. But the "fossil fuels" – oil, coal and gas – are running out, and so we are looking for ways of using solar energy. In the future it will become more important.

Catching the sun

Houses that trap the sun's rays are not new. The ancient Greeks and Romans warmed their homes in this way. Many houses today are heated by the same method, making the maximum use of the sun's rays to directly heat the rooms and provide hot water.

The house in the diagram and the photograph opposite has large windows to trap the sun. Its walls and floors are made from thick brick which holds the heat, and keeps the house warm at night when temperatures fall.

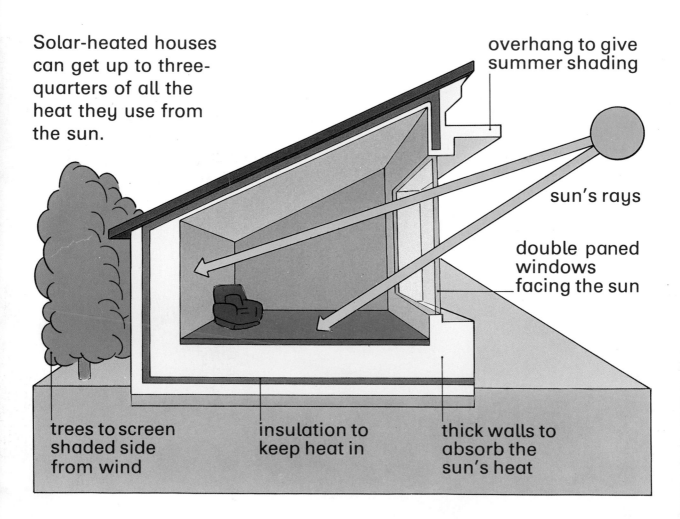

Solar-heated houses can get up to three-quarters of all the heat they use from the sun.

overhang to give summer shading

sun's rays

double paned windows facing the sun

trees to screen shaded side from wind

insulation to keep heat in

thick walls to absorb the sun's heat

The windows in this house have two panes of glass to stop heat escaping, similar to storm windows. Thick insulation material in the roof and walls keeps warm air in the house.

The coldest side of the house is protected by trees. Because the house could get very hot in the summer, an overhang shades the sunniest windows. "Energy saving" houses built like this even work well in cool countries like Sweden. However, buildings without special features also get around 15 percent of their heat from the sun.

A simple source

Some people fit a very simple solar collector to their houses by replacing some of the roof tiles with glass or plastic sheets. The sheets trap warm air in the roof; this is then circulated around the house by electric fans. All the drafty places around windows are sealed up.

Automatic controls can also be fitted which switch off the lights and household appliances when they are not being used. Simple improvements like this save energy and help to conserve precious gas and electricity.

Saving on the grid – flat plate collectors

Quite ordinary homes can be easily converted to use solar energy by installing a simple "active" heating system.

A "flat plate" solar collector is fitted to the roof. This is a rectangular box, painted black on one side. Black surfaces absorb energy very well, and convert sunlight into heat easily. Cold water is pumped through tubes in front of the black plate and is warmed up. The hot water can then be used for washing, cooking or heating the rooms.

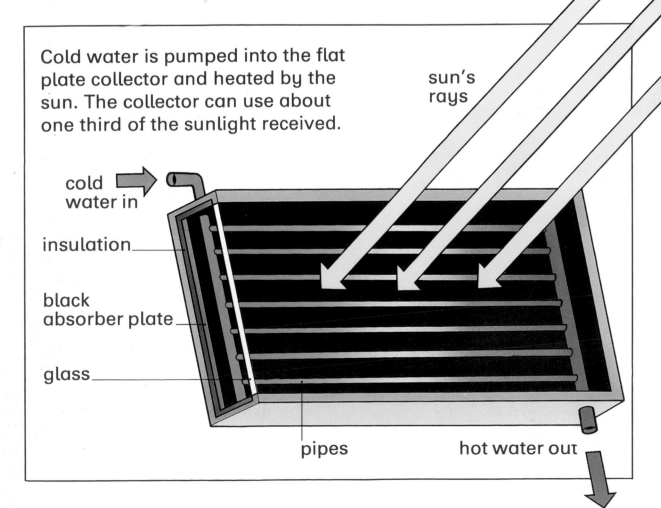

Cold water is pumped into the flat plate collector and heated by the sun. The collector can use about one third of the sunlight received.

sun's rays

cold water in

insulation

black absorber plate

glass

pipes

hot water out

Tracking the sun

Most solar collectors can generate much higher temperatures than the flat plate "black box." "Sun-tracking" collectors, which can move and follow the path of the sun, have a greater output of heat. Sometimes the actual tracking motor is solar-powered.

This Swiss chalet has its own sun-tracking collector. The part that reflects the sun's rays is called a "parabolic trough." The sun's rays are reflected from the trough's shiny surface onto a heat-absorbing tube in the center; inside, water or other liquids can be heated to temperatures of 300°C (572°F).

sun morning

noon

cold water

hot water

afternoon

By following the sun's course across the sky, parabolic collectors get the benefit of the sun's direct rays all day long.

Dish collectors

The large parabolic – or dish – collector in this photograph uses the sun's rays to make steam and so generate electricity. It works by directing them onto one single spot – the "focus point."

The collector tracks the sun's path across the sky, and its shiny surfaces concentrate the sun's power onto a mirror. The mirror bounces the sunlight back through a hole at the base of the collector. This heats liquid in a "closed system," which in turn boils water to make steam. It is this steam which drives a turbine to generate electricity.

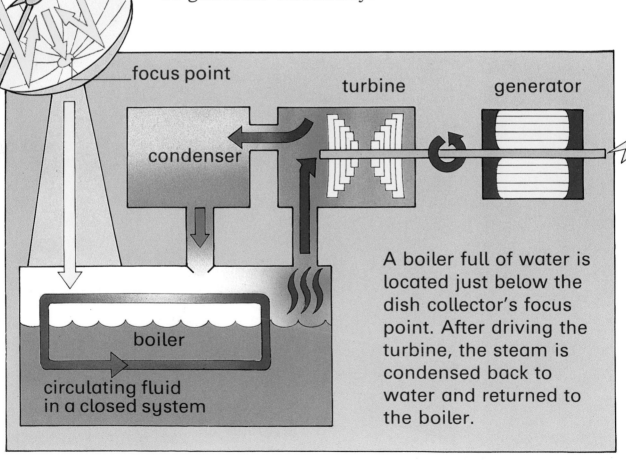

mirror

focus point

turbine

generator

condenser

boiler

circulating fluid in a closed system

A boiler full of water is located just below the dish collector's focus point. After driving the turbine, the steam is condensed back to water and returned to the boiler.

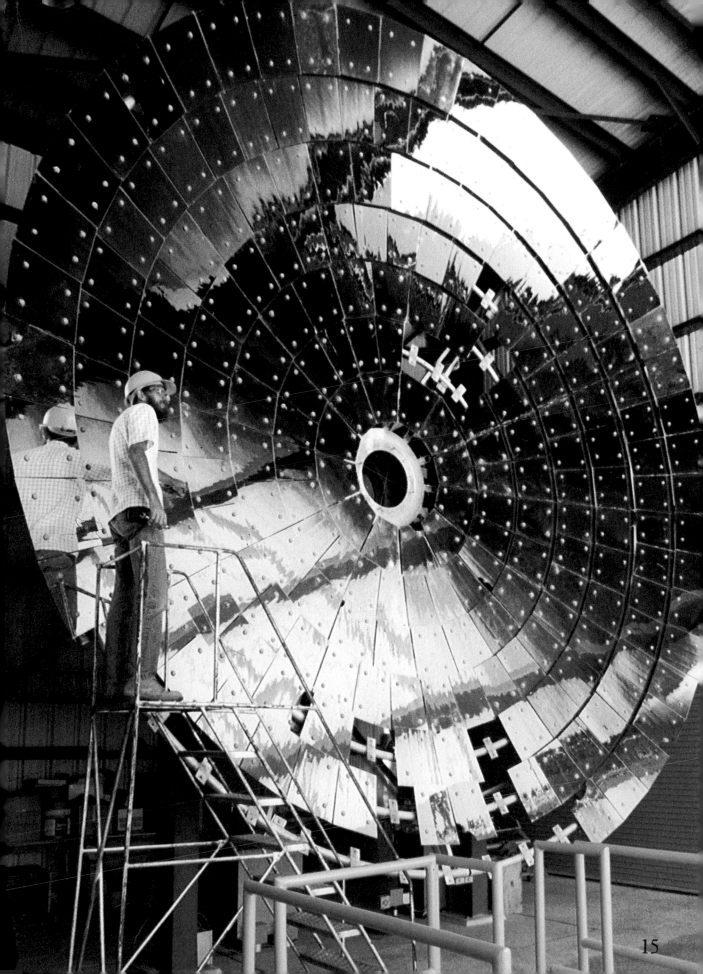

Power towers

Hundreds, sometimes thousands, of mirrors are used to gather the sun's rays in a type of power station called a "power tower." One of the biggest has been built as an experiment; it is in New Mexico, and has 1,775 mirrors. These are all focused on a boiler at the top of a 60 meter (200 foot) tower.

However, solar power stations make most of their electricity when the weather is sunny – and when we need it least! So a lot is wasted since it has to be changed into heat, stored, and then changed back when it is needed.

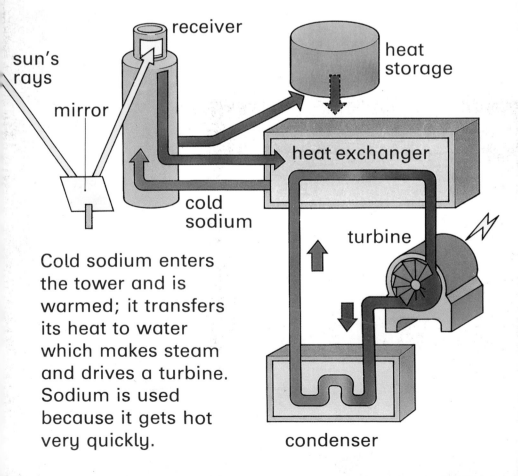

Cold sodium enters the tower and is warmed; it transfers its heat to water which makes steam and drives a turbine. Sodium is used because it gets hot very quickly.

The five megawatt power tower,
Albuquerque, New Mexico.

17

The furnace

In the Pyrenees Mountains of France, a huge experimental solar furnace has been built. It is situated high up in the mountains to avoid polluted air and smoke, and to get the full force of the sun's rays.

The huge, shiny reflector is made from hundreds of small mirrors. The solar furnace – with its focus point – is housed in the tower.

The solar furnace can produce temperatures of 3,000°C (5,432°F). This is high enough to melt certain metals, and makes experiments on rare elements possible. The research work that is carried out in the solar furnace is used in the French space program.

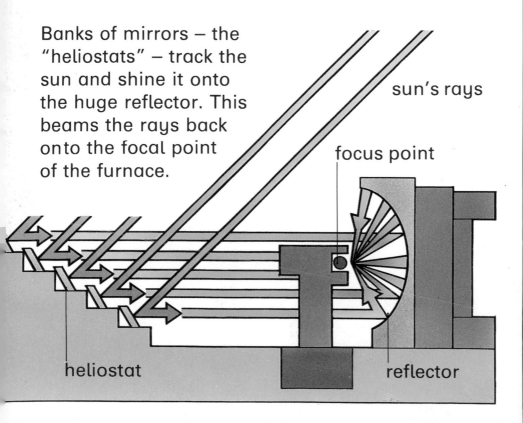

Banks of mirrors – the "heliostats" – track the sun and shine it onto the huge reflector. This beams the rays back onto the focal point of the furnace.

sun's rays

focus point

heliostat

reflector

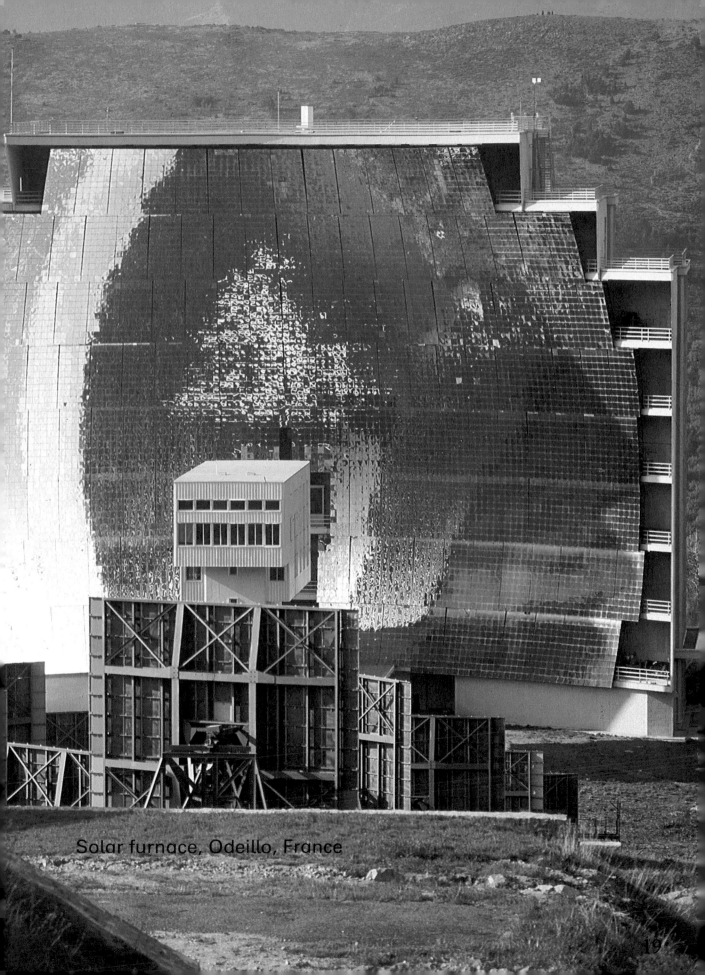
Solar furnace, Odeillo, France

Solar cells

Tiny slivers of silicon, coated with special chemicals, form the basis of the solar or "photovoltaic" cell. The solar cell can actually capture the rays of the sun and turn them *directly* into electricity.

When sunlight falls on the cell, electrons are released and they flow across the chemical layers on its surface, producing a small current. Solar cells convert about one sixth of the energy they receive into useful electrical energy. But many solar cells used together can make a great deal of power. The photograph shows giant panels of them in use at a large power plant in New Mexico.

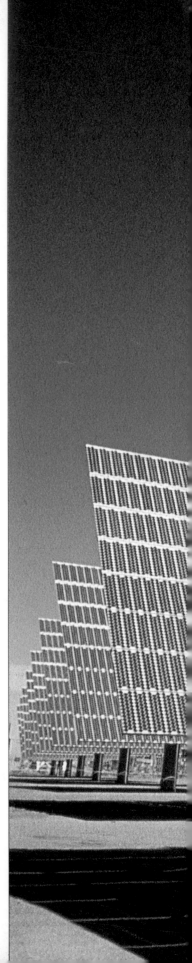

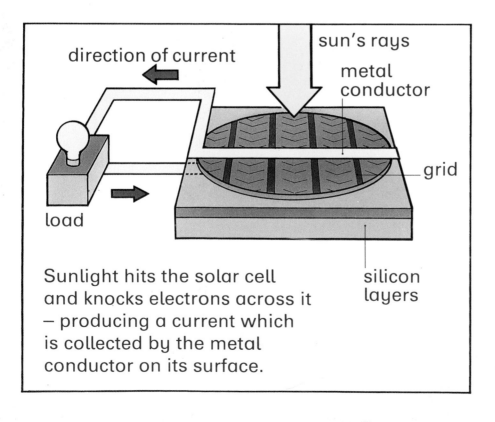

Sunlight hits the solar cell and knocks electrons across it – producing a current which is collected by the metal conductor on its surface.

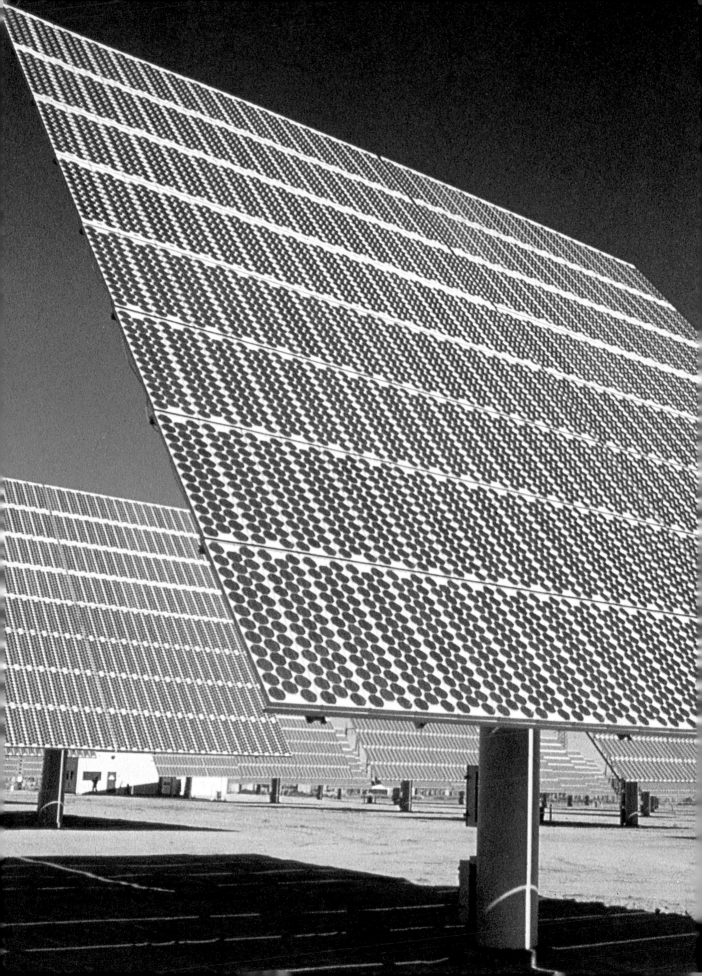

Transport

Did you know that solar cells can be used to power most types of transport – from boats to bicycles to aircraft?

In 1981 the "Solar Challenger" was the first solar-powered aircraft to cross the English Channel; its solar cells were lent by NASA.

Solar cells work really well in space. The sun shines all the time, and there are no clouds to block out its rays. In spacecraft, panels of solar cells are used to generate up to 4,000 kilowatts of power.

The Solar Challenger got its power from 16,000 solar cells which were glued to its wings and tail.

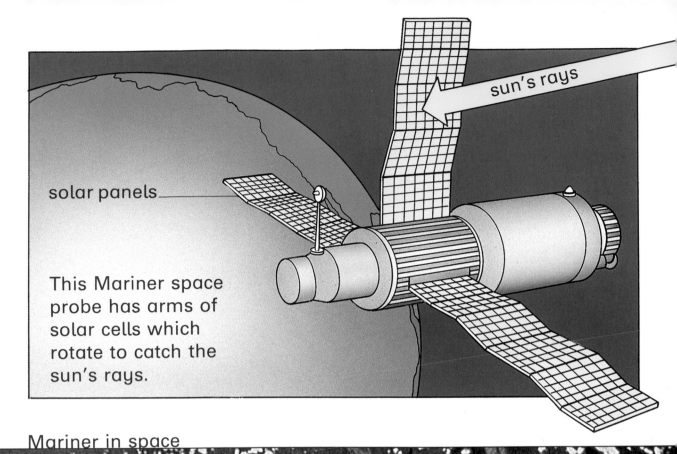

solar panels

This Mariner space probe has arms of solar cells which rotate to catch the sun's rays.

sun's rays

Mariner in space

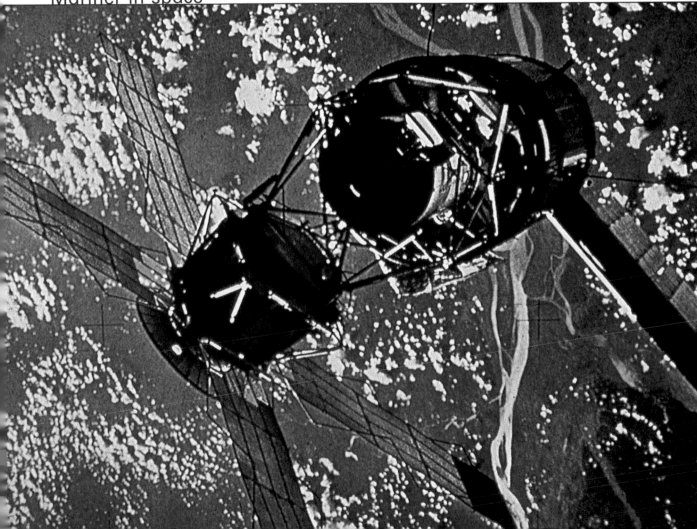

Solar ponds

Special "solar ponds" are also used to trap the sun's heat. The pond has sloping sides and a flat bottom which is painted black. It is filled with salt water which will absorb heat.

The salt drifts down through the pond so that the saltiest layer lies just above the black bottom. When the sun shines, the temperature in the bottom of the pond can rise up to 90°C (194°F).

Hot salt water is pumped from the pond to a boiler. It transfers its heat to fresh water in the boiler, which produces steam and drives a turbine. The steam is then cooled back to water by cold salt water from the pond.

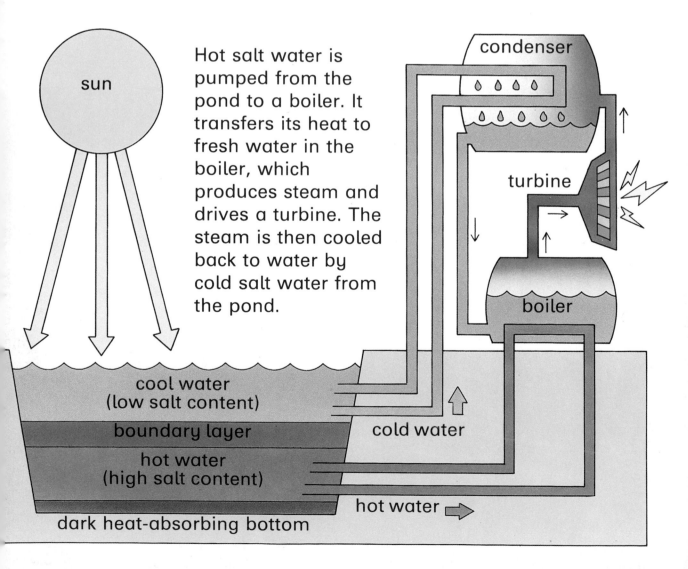

sun

condenser

turbine

boiler

cool water
(low salt content)

boundary layer

hot water
(high salt content)

cold water

dark heat-absorbing bottom

hot water

In future, it may be possible to use the oceans as giant solar collectors. In some hot places, sea water is warmed by the sun to temperatures as high as 25°C (77°F) – hot enough to drive special turbines. Experiments with these are now being carried out.

One day, giant panels of solar cells might even be set up in space to beam their energy down to collectors on Earth.

The biggest solar collector?

Fact file 1

Simple solar collectors can be very effective. Small solar ponds are cheap and efficient and can even be fitted to rooftops! The compound parabolic reflector is a simple version of the bigger parabolic trough, and is often used to heat greenhouses.

Sun-tracking collectors can give much higher temperatures than simple collectors, but they are more expensive to install and run. Many simple collectors spread over a wide area can produce more heat than sun-tracking collectors for the same amount of money.

Stationary collectors		Temperature range
Solar pond		86 to 194°F
Flat plate		86 to 194°F
Vacuum tube		122 to 392°F
Compound parabolic		158 to 482°F

Sun-tracking collectors		Temperature range
Parabolic trough		158 to 572°F
Parabolic dish		392 to 1,652°F
Power tower		392 to 2,552°F

A vacuum tube is a special kind of stationary solar collector which works in a similar way to a thermos flask.

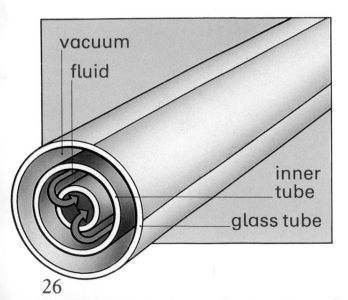

vacuum

fluid

inner tube

glass tube

Water in the central tubes is warmed to temperatures of 200°C (392°F). The heat does not escape because the tubes are in a vacuum.

The Egyptian government has set up a project which uses vacuum tubes. They drive heat pumps and make electricity for remote areas. The project is called "King Tut;" it is named after the Egyptian pharaoh, Tutankhamun, whose followers worshipped the sun.

Did you know that Africa has the world's first solar-powered hospital? It is in Mali, on the edge of the Sahara Desert, and so is well placed to make use of solar power. Energy gathered by solar cells powers fans, air conditioning in intensive care units, radiotherapy machines, water pumps and other vital equipment.

Many household machines can be powered by solar energy — refrigerators, TV sets and cooking stoves are among them.

Some countries even use solar cells to power their telephones. Both Jordan and Niger use solar power for telecommunications.

In China you can take a "solar bath" on a train! The arid Xinkiang region has a "bath train" which uses solar-heated water; it goes up and down the Xinkiang-Lanzhou railroad, providing baths for the railroad workers and people who live in the vicinity.

Drinking water is in short supply in many parts of the world. But in Greece, the USSR and Saudi Arabia the sun is used to turn sea water into drinking water.

Sea water is poured into tanks painted black to absorb the heat. Sloping panes of glass are then placed on top. The sun's heat makes the water evaporate and it condenses on the glass, leaving the salt on the tank. Fresh water runs down the panes into troughs.

A solar "distillation plant"

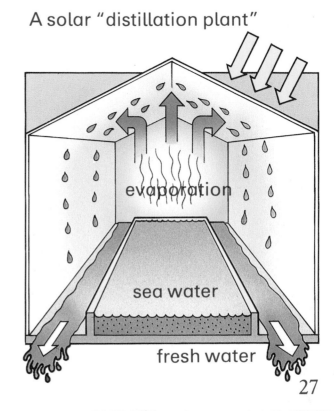

evaporation

sea water

fresh water

Fact file 2

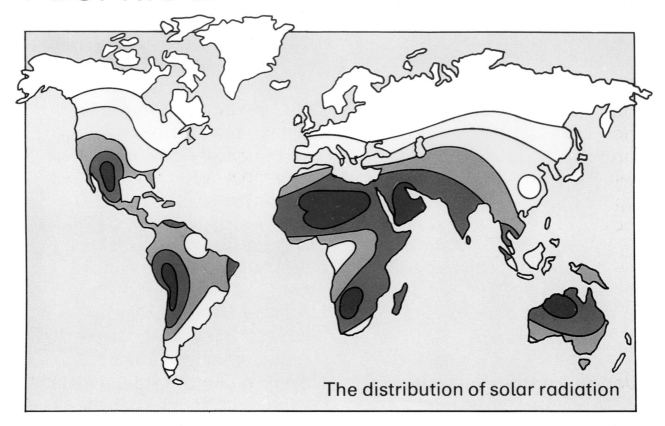

The distribution of solar radiation

The map shows how the sun's rays fall unevenly on the Earth. The red areas get the most sun, with average daytime summer temperatures in excess of 30°C (86°F).

Most of the very sunny areas are deserts, waste lands or thinly populated countries. These places receive huge amounts of solar energy.

But the whole planet gets more energy from the sun than from all other fuels put together — enough to power 40,000 fans for each person in the world.

Australia gets 28,000 times more energy — in the form of sunshine — than it uses each year. But even a cool country like the UK gets 80 times more sunshine energy than its large population can use.

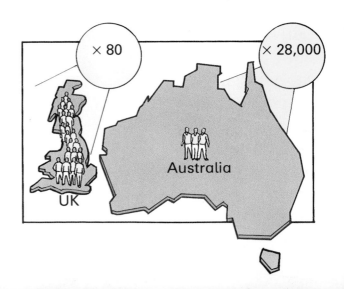

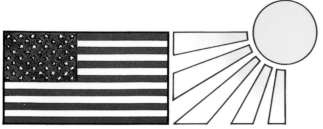

The USA spends more money than any other country on solar power. While some is used to provide remote communities with electricity, much more is spent on big projects, such as power towers.

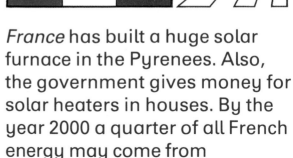

France has built a huge solar furnace in the Pyrenees. Also, the government gives money for solar heaters in houses. By the year 2000 a quarter of all French energy may come from "renewable" sources.

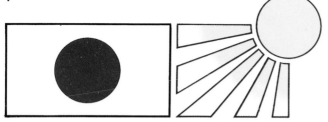

Japan has started a programme called "Project Sunshine." It includes plans for an 800 mirror solar furnace. Manufacture of solar collectors is now high in Japan and they are installed in many homes.

Spain plans to build three large solar power stations in the mountains, to provide isolated villages with electricity. Spain is also cooperating with the USA in the construction of a one megawatt solar furnace.

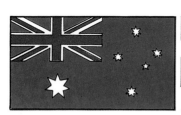

Australia has its own "Solar City" – a purpose-built area in Brisbane. It has solar-heated houses, swimming pools and barbecues. Throughout the country, sales of solar heaters are high.

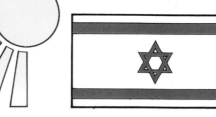

Israel saves $2 million each year by using solar energy. 20% of the country's homes use it for heating water, and there are plans to put rooftop solar ponds in new houses and factories and other buildings.

Glossary

Active solar-heating   The action of gathering up the sun's rays in collectors and using them for heating.

Flat plate collector   A simple solar collector; water is pumped into it and is heated by the sun.

Generator   The part of a power station that converts mechanical power into electricity.

Heliostats   Banks of mirrors which turn during the day and follow the sun's path.

Passive solar-heating   When buildings are designed to capture and use the sun's rays.

Photovoltaic cell   The technical name for a solar cell.

Reflector   The shiny surface of a solar collector.

Solar pond   A pond which absorbs the heat of the sun. The hot water can be used directly, or used to generate electricity.

Sun-tracking collectors   Collectors which move and follow the sun's path during the day.

Watt   The unit for measuring electrical power. A lightbulb might use 60 or 100 watts of electricity. A kilowatt (kw) equals 1,000 watts, a megawatt (mw) one million.

Index

Acknowledgements
The publishers wish to thank the following people and organizations who have helped in the preparation of this book:
Friends of the Earth; Christian Aid; Geoffrey Barnard (Earthscan); Energy Technology Support Unit (ETSU, Harwell); Lucas Energy Systems; Sandia National Laboratories USA; SERI (Solar Energy Research Institute) USA; Shell Briefing Service UK; Sir William Halcrow Ltd.

Typeset by Dorchester Typesetting